NATIONAL GEOGRAPHIC KiDS

DOGGY DEFENDERS

WILLOW

★ ★ ★

THE THERAPY DOG

Lisa M. Gerry

Photographs by Lori Epstein

NATIONAL GEOGRAPHIC

SCHOLASTIC INC.

Meet WILLOW!

Willow is a rescued greyhound. Greyhounds have long bodies and pointy snouts, which help them run really fast.

She lives with her best friend, Megan.

Willow loves to relax
at home and nap.

But she also works
really hard: She has a job!

Willow is a therapy dog.

She knows how to make
people smile and helps them
feel better if they are sad.

Every morning, Willow gets ready for work. Her good friend Jim helps her get dressed.

Willow wears a **bright red vest** to let people know that she is a therapy dog.

Every day on the job is different for Willow.

Today, she is going to visit a hospital.

Inside the hospital, Megan and
Willow join some more of their friends:
other therapy dogs!

They all work together to help sick people feel better.

Willow and her friends visit the patients.

Willow is very gentle.

She lies close so people can pet her.

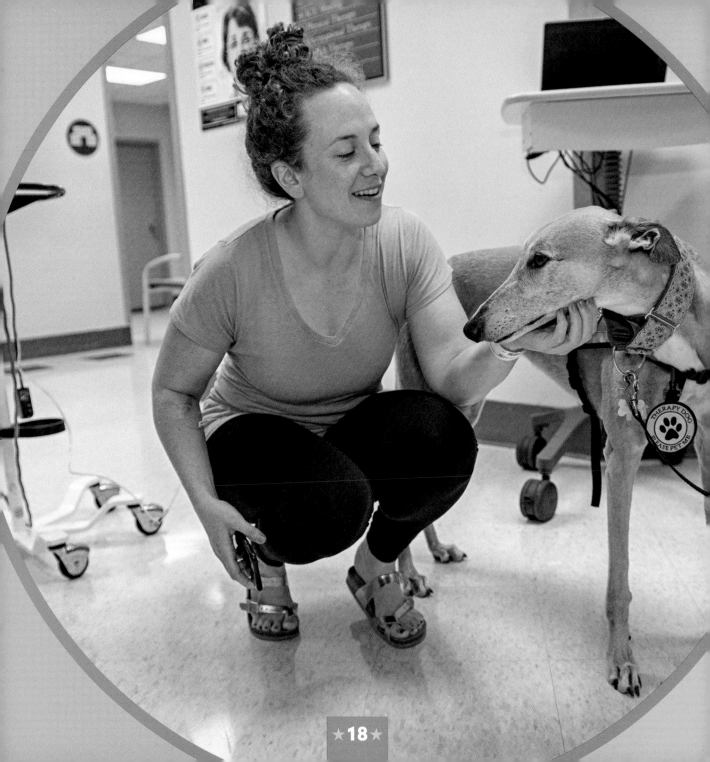

Willow makes people smile.

Great job, Willow.

Willow also visits the doctors and nurses to thank them for their hard work.

They love seeing Willow!

Now it's time for Willow's next visit.

Willow and Megan are going to visit a **school**. There, Willow will help the busy students feel happy and relaxed.

Everyone gives Willow
kisses and hugs.

She brings big smiles
to their faces.

Next, Willow
and Megan head to
a home for retired
veterans.

Veterans are people who have served in the military.

They pet Willow's soft fur and scratch behind her ears.

Willow has brightened their day.

Now Willow and Megan have one more stop to make. They are visiting a library!

Willow will help kids practice reading.

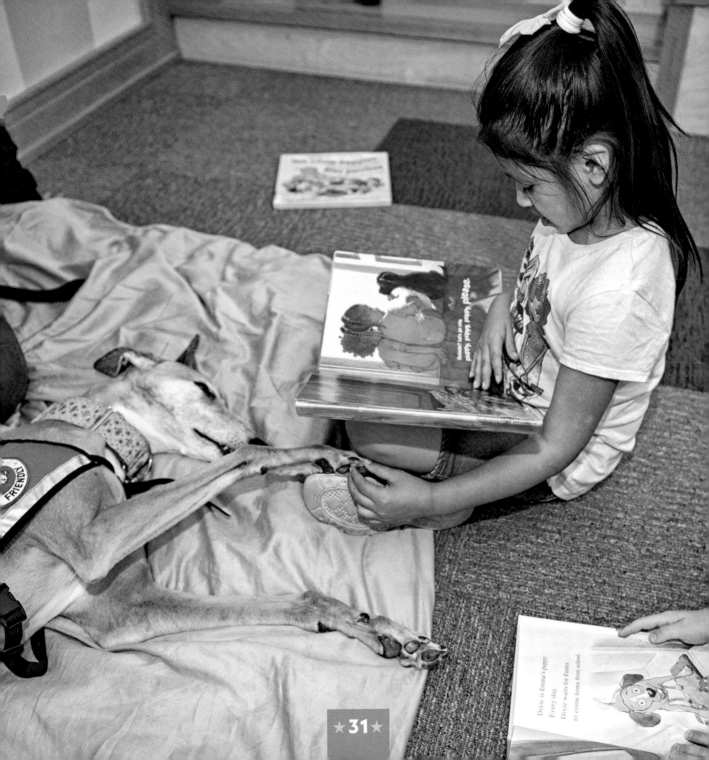

The kids
love reading to
Willow. She is a
great listener!

Phew, what a long day—now it's time to relax! Willow spends her free time making new friends ...

Willow

... snacking on special treats ...

... and cuddling!

But even when she's not working, Willow doesn't stop making people smile.

She makes Jim smile. She makes Megan smile. And they make her smile, too!

Now, after a long day
and lots of fun, it's time
for bed. Megan helps
Willow put on her pajamas.

Cozy!

Good night, Willow!

Thank you for helping.

Meet the Team!

Megan answers questions about Willow and helping their community.

Q How did you get Willow?

A I adopted Willow from Second Chance Greyhounds (SCG), a greyhound rescue organization located in Georgia. SCG finds homes for former racing greyhounds.

Q Who trained Willow?

A Willow learned basic skills with Second Chance Greyhounds. We passed the AKC Canine Good Citizen test and then we became a certified therapy team with People. Animals. Love. (PAL).

Q What do you and Willow do in your free time?

A Willow and I love to go for car rides together and play upbeat music—Willow looks out the windows and bobs her head to the music. She also enjoys going out to eat with me and her dog sister, Pumpkin.

Q **What is Willow's favorite toy?**

A Willow has a big stuffed dog named Uga that she cuddles and sleeps on during the afternoon. She also likes to take my shoes—not to chew them but to sleep with them.

Q **What is the best part of owning a therapy dog?**

A I love experiencing the amazing and unique ability that animals have to heal people. It's a blessing to see and feel while watching Willow working.

Willow's Tips on Being a Good Friend and Neighbor

Willow works hard to make people happy. Here's how you can help make people smile, too!

1. **Volunteer! Ask a parent to help you spend time with a local charity or group.**

2. **Be there for your friends and loved ones when they need it.**

3. **Talk, share, and listen to friends and family.**

4. **Respect others: Respect people and your differences.**

5. **Always ask permission before approaching or petting a dog.**

6. **Use your manners: Say please and thank you.**

7. **If you are getting a pet, try adopting one from a shelter.**

8. **Donate the toys and books you don't want anymore.**

ISBN 978-1-338-65267-3

12 11 10 9 8 7 6 5 4 3 2   20 21 22 23 24 25

Printed in the U.S.A.   40

First Scholastic printing, February 2020

Book design by Callie Broaddus

The publisher would like to thank Lisa Gerry, author; Lori Epstein, photographer; Paige Towler, project editor; Shannon Hibberd, photo editor; and Willow, Megan, Jim, George Washington University Hospital, Lt. Joseph P. Kenney Institute, Garfield Elementary School, Armed Forces Retirement Home, PAL (People. Animals. Love.), Mt. Pleasant Library, and Hero Dogs for their support and dedication to their communities.